N MENTAL HEALTH™

teen stress and anxiety

Jason Porterfield

ROSEN
PUBLISHING®

New York

Published in 2014 by The Rosen Publishing Group, Inc.
29 East 21st Street, New York, NY 10010

First Edition

Library of Congress Cataloging-in-Publication Data

Porterfield, Jason.
Teen stress and anxiety/Jason Porterfield.
    pages cm.–(Teen mental health)
Includes bibliographical references and index.
ISBN 978-1-4777-1751-6 (library binding)
1. Stress in adolescence. 2. Anxiety in adolescence. I. Title.
BF724.3.S86P67 2014
155.5'1246–dc23

        2013021778

Manufactured in the United States of America

CPSIA Compliance Information: Batch #W14YA: For further information, contact Rosen Publishing, New York, New York, at 1-800-237-9932.

contents

chapter one

Understanding Stress

Modern human beings live in stressful times. Many people experience ongoing frustrations, pressures, and conflicts that cause constant feelings of tension and unease. Common sources of stress include concerns over money, work, school, health, relationships, and family. People feeling stressed often say they have more to do than they can handle. The idea of stress is a recent concept, and scientific studies of the consequences of stress only began in the mid-twentieth century. Researchers have since learned that stress can significantly impact physical and mental health. Small doses of stress can be beneficial, providing motivation to meet a challenge. Chronic stress, however, can cause health problems and contribute to psychological conditions such as anxiety or depression.

Each individual responds differently to stressful situations. A teenager may experience minimal stress over a big test but feel utterly stressed out before a first date. Some people can tolerate long-term stress better than others. Fortunately, there are ways to reduce the effects of stress. Each person will have to try various techniques to find what works best, but taking the time to relieve stress is worth the effort.

Stressed or Anxious?

Stress and anxiety are not the same feeling, though they are related. Stress is primarily a physical and mental response to threats, pressures, and demands. The heart rate increases and palms get sweaty. The mind has difficulty concentrating.

Anxiety includes emotional and cognitive symptoms in addition to physical and mental responses. People experiencing anxiety are worried and fearful. They tend to overthink and obsess on the source of the anxiety. Anxiety is often a result of stress, but additional factors can lead to anxiety. Some personality types are more prone to anxiety, and some people have a family history of anxiety. Health conditions and substance abuse can also cause anxiety. A

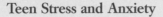

Teens can experience stress triggered by many sources, from the everyday pressures of school, work, and family routines to traumatic life events.

traumatic event can produce anxiety.

Stress and anxiety are often associated with another condition: depression. People suffering from depression suffer persistent feelings of sadness, low self-esteem, and a loss of interest in favorite activities or hobbies. Stress contributes to both anxiety and depression by affecting how the brain processes critical situations. People who suffer from either anxiety or depression tend to overestimate the risks of stressful situations and underestimate their ability to cope. Depression and anxiety share some symptoms, such as irritability, trouble concentrating, and physical symptoms such as headaches.

Anxiety and depression are sometimes said to be flip sides of the same coin. For some, stress causes anxiety, which in turn leads to depression. According to *Psychology Today*, between 60 and 70 percent of people suffering from major depression also have an anxiety disorder. Half of those with anxiety also show symptoms of depression. People experiencing both depression and anxiety have more severe symptoms and more trouble responding to treatment.

Responding to Stress

Stress is the body's reaction to a trigger–or stressor–such as a threat or high-pressure situation. The response to an immediate threat is called acute stress. The brain and body react automatically with a fight-or-flight response to the perceived danger.

To generate the stress response, the brain activates systems that send out neurotransmitters. As a result, hormones such as cortisol and adrenaline produce physical changes in the body. Heart rate and blood pressure increase. The circulatory system directs blood to major muscle groups, which is why your hands might feel cold when you're extremely nervous. The pupils of the eyes dilate to let in more light and improve vision. Muscles tense and levels of glucose in the blood increase to give the body more energy. The immune system diverts its defenses to areas of the body that could be affected in a physical confrontation, such as the skin and lymph nodes. The digestive system shuts down to allow increased activity in other systems of the body. The mind has difficulty focusing on details because a potential threat could come from any direction.

Once the threat has passed, the relaxation response kicks in. The body's systems and hormonal balance return to normal.

7

The fight-or-flight response gave early humans an evolutionary advantage in an environment where people were surrounded by physical dangers. It quickly put the body in peak condition to react. In the modern world, however, the stress response is often less beneficial. Stressors are less likely to be an attacking predator and more likely to be homework, deadlines, and bills. Unlike physical threats, which abate quickly, these stressors can be ongoing.

When Stress Starts to Hurt

Acute stress is an isolated, short-term incident. Today, people can be bombarded by near-constant sources of stress. For some, this may result in episodic acute stress, in which one critical situation always seems followed by another.

An additional harmful type of stress occurs when an individual experiences ongoing pressure that keeps the fight-or-flight response in a constant state of activation. This condition is known as chronic stress. It disrupts some of the systems of the body, causing numerous health problems and exacerbating others. According to WebMD, between 75 and 90 percent of all physicians' office visits are for stress-related problems.

Chronic stress weakens the immune system, which defends against disease. People who experience chronic stress are more vulnerable to infections. Chronic stress may also worsen allergies, asthma, and autoimmune diseases.

Acute stress affects the circulatory system, digestive system, and respiratory system. Chronic stress has been linked to illnesses related to these systems. Symptoms include shortness of breath, tight or aching muscles, problems sleeping, and heartburn. Chronic stress also contributes to skin ailments such as eczema, an itchy inflammation. Over the long term, stress may increase the risk of conditions such as high blood pressure, heart disease, and stroke. In addition, chronic stress worsens diseases such as diabetes and cancer. Because stress affects concentration, people who experience chronic stress may have memory problems.

Stress causes psychological distress in addition to physical symptoms. As mentioned previously, stress contributes to anxiety and depression. People sometimes deal with stress and its psychological consequences in unhealthy ways. Some turn to food for relief, and stress is frequently linked to obesity. Individuals experiencing stress may also be more prone to substance abuse.

Stressful Situations

There are several different broad categories of stress. People experience traumatic stress in life-threatening situations such as an assault or a natural disaster. Major life changes, such as getting married or dealing with personal loss, also cause considerable stress as people adapt to their new circumstances. Another category is routine stress, which can lead to symptoms of chronic stress.

A 2012 report by the American Psychiatric Association found that most Americans–69 percent of all adults–considered money to be the greatest source of stress in their lives. Other major sources of stress included work, the economy, family responsibilities, relationships,

Parental stress and conflicts can take a toll on kids and adolescents. Many parents don't realize how strongly their stress and anxiety affects the whole family.

family health problems, and personal health concerns. Most of these sources of stress involve ongoing issues that are likely to contribute to chronic stress. Overscheduling and multitasking can keep people in a constant state of stress response. It's easy to underestimate the gradually developing health consequences of routine stress and ignore minor symptoms such as headaches or a constant feeling of being overwhelmed.

The American Psychiatric Association report also found that women experienced higher levels of stress than men, and they were more likely to say that stress had been increasing in their lives over the past five years. Men and women also manage stress differently. Generally, women are inclined to "tend and befriend" by nurturing people around them and engaging in social activities. Men react with the fight-or-flight response by retaliating or trying to escape from stress.

Older Americans generally experienced less stress than younger generations. Mature Americans (born before 1945) reported an average stress level of 3.7 on a 10-point scale. Millennials (born between 1980 and 1996) reported a level of 5.4 and were more likely to say that stress had been increasing in their lives. The APA report did not examine teen stress, but high school students have also been reporting increasing levels of stress. Their main sources of stress are schoolwork and high pressure to achieve.

Each individual responds to stress differently. One person might thrive in a high-pressure work environment, while another becomes overwhelmed. People with type A personalities often create ongoing stressful situations in their own lives. Some people tend toward perfectionism or get disturbed over minor stressors. Others are naturally more laid-back and less susceptible to the effects of stress.

chapter two

Understandin Anxiety

Everybody knows the signs of anxiety. You've got a big exam coming up, and you're already worried about it a week in advance. You start thinking through every possible scenario in which things could go wrong. When you finally sit down at your desk on the day of the exam, the palms of your hands are sweaty and you've got butterflies in your stomach. A dose of normal anxiety in such a situation might help your performance. It prompts you to study beforehand and focus your efforts during the exam. Excessive anxiety, however, can have consequences on your day-to-day life. If you neglect other activities because of anxiety, or if anxiety makes you irritable or continually apprehensive, it could be a problem that you should address.

If you suffer from an anxiety disorder, you're not alone. Anxiety disorders are the most common form of mental illness in the United States. According to the National Institute of Mental Health (NIMH), about forty million adult Americans are affected by anxiety disorders. In addition, about 8 percent of teens between the ages of thirteen and eighteen have an anxiety disorder. People with anxiety disorders respond well to treatment, but only about a third of adults and 18 percent of teens who suffer from an anxiety disorder seek treatment. Without treatment, anxiety disorders often get worse.

Recognizing Anxiety

People suffering from severe anxiety or an anxiety disorder don't always realize that anxiety is the root cause of their symptoms. You probably associate anxiety with the general symptoms of a condition called generalized anxiety disorder (GAD)–persistent and intense tension and worry. But anxiety disorders include a spectrum of conditions. People experiencing chest pain are sometimes suffering panic attacks, the primary symptom of panic disorder. People who suffer from social anxiety disorder often believe they're just shy. Conditions such as phobias and

Anxiety can have its roots in many different factors, including stressful events, environment, genetics, underlying health problems, and substance abuse.

obsessive-compulsive disorders fall into the category of anxiety disorders.

In addition, people sometimes doubt that they suffer from an anxiety disorder because they can't identify a specific cause, such as a traumatic event or excessive stress. However, anxiety often occurs without being triggered by a specific event. A number of sources other than stress or life events can cause anxiety. There is a genetic factor to anxiety, meaning that it tends to run in families. The activity of neurotransmitters in the brain contributes to anxiety.

Illnesses, substance abuse, and environmental factors can affect anxiety as well.

Teenagers, in particular, should be aware of the symptoms of anxiety and anxiety disorders. Many mental illnesses, including anxiety disorders, tend to develop during adolescence.

Symptoms of Anxiety

The American Psychiatric Association defines anxiety as "an emotion characterized by feelings of tension, worried thoughts and physical changes like increased blood pressure." Anxiety often involves the same physical symptoms as the fight-or-flight response to stress. But anxiety also includes emotional, behavioral, and cognitive elements.

The primary emotion behind anxiety disorders is fear. When you're stressed, you're reacting to a real fear–a barking dog, talking in front of the entire class, worrying about a health condition. When you're anxious, you're anticipating future dangers that probably won't ever occur. People suffering from anxiety tend to worry that any situation will end in the worst possible outcome. They are often beset with feelings of hopelessness, nervousness, apprehension, and restlessness.

The emotional aspect of anxiety often influences people's behavioral and cognitive responses. People know that their fears and worries are irrational, but they can't help their reactions. One common behavioral response is avoidance of objects and situations that trigger anxiety. Cognitive responses include persistent worry, rumination (overthinking), and obsessions.

15

For some teens, reading a paper in front of the class is no big deal. For others, public speaking represents an overwhelming source of anxiety.

Special Concerns for Teens

Ongoing research is constantly improving the understanding of the causes, diagnosis, treatment, and prevention of anxiety disorders and other mental illnesses. Anxiety is a complex issue, with numerous contributing factors and possible courses of progression. Scientists are learning more about how stress, fear, and anxiety work in the brain.

Such research could open up new means of treatment for anxiety disorders.

Researchers are increasingly recognizing that a teenager's brain works differently from an adult brain. Teenagers do not experience anxiety disorders and other mental health issues in the same way that adults do. Medications may have different effects on teens than on adults or even children.

The brain undergoes a major reorganization process from the early teens to the mid-twenties. This period of development explains some teen behaviors that often confound adults, such as taking risks and acting impulsively. Teens process information differently from adults and may be more likely to make decisions based on emotions without weighing consequences. Hormonal changes, which include activity of stress hormones, also affect behavior. Research has shown that teenagers may be more vulnerable to stress and anxiety than adults because the teenage brain processes fear differently.

Adolescence is also the period of development when teens mature socially and begin mapping out long-term career plans. Teens begin taking on more responsibilities and making more decisions. Yet some key sources of stress and anxiety—such as money matters, family conflicts, and major changes like moving to a new city—are beyond a teen's control. Teens may also face sources of stress specific to adolescence, such as peer pressure, bullying, too much homework, issues with parents, a first breakup, starting out a new school year or moving to a new school, and

Teens may respond to anxiety by withdrawing from friends and social activities, a reaction that can make the situation worse and lead to a personal crisis.

meeting the demands related to grades and extracurricular activities.

It's sometimes hard for adults to relate to the stress and anxiety experienced by today's overscheduled, interconnected teenagers. Parents might overlook signs of a teen's problem with anxiety by attributing symptoms to the ordinary pressures of high school. Good communication will increase the likelihood that either a parent or a teen will recognize and address concerns about anxiety before they develops into a serious illness.

MYTHS AND FACTS

Myth: Stress and anxiety are always bad.

Fact: Under some circumstances, stress and anxiety can provide energy and initiative. The stress response can improve athletic performance during an important game, for example, and reasonable anxiety might spur you to study for a big exam. When stress or anxiety starts to interfere with your day-to-day functioning, however, you need to take steps to get it under control.

Myth: Stress affects everybody in the same way.

Fact: Different people get stressed out by different sources of stress. Some people are naturally more resilient under stress than others. Likewise, different people find a variety of techniques that are effective for managing stress.

Myth: Anxiety is all in your head, and if you just try hard enough, you can get over it.

Fact: Anxiety disorders are mental illnesses that cause intense suffering and can negatively impact one's school, family, and social life. They are serious medical conditions that respond to proven courses of treatment administered by professionals.

Stress and Anxiety Disorders

It's normal to experi-
ence occasional
moments of anxiety in
day-to-day life. Some
anxiety can even be beneficial because it can act as a
source of motivation. When
anxiety turns into excessive
fear with no specific
source, however, it could
indicate an anxiety disorder.

Symptoms of
anxiety disorders
resemble extreme
versions of ordi-
nary anxiety.
There are six
types of anxiety
disorder:

- It's typical to experience anxiety about upcoming major events, but constant gnawing anxiety with no specific cause could be a symptom of *generalized anxiety disorder* (GAD).
- Everyone feels slightly nervous and jumpy immediately before an exam or a big game, but sudden unexpected bouts of terror could be a symptom of *panic disorder.*
- It's common to have routines and appreciate cleanliness and order, but uncontrollable ritual actions and out-of-control cleaning could be symptoms of *obsessive-compulsive disorder* (OCD).
- Shyness and awkwardness about social situations is normal, but if you're too nervous to face everyday social situations, they could be symptoms of *social anxiety disorder.*
- Many people are mildly fearful of the dark or heights or spiders, but an extreme paralyzing fear of a certain object or situation could be a *specific phobia.*
- It's typical to be distraught after a traumatic event, but if the memories and ongoing response become overwhelming, it could be a symptom of *post-traumatic stress disorder* (PTSD).

If an anxiety disorder begins to interfere with your everyday life, you should seek professional help. Anxiety disorders can be managed, and treatment can help people overcome the fear and obstacles associated with anxiety.

Generalized Anxiety Disorder (GAD)

Generalized anxiety disorder (GAD) is marked by chronic, persistent anxiety over issues both large and small. People with GAD worry constantly about what could go wrong and anticipate disaster at every turn. They often recognize that the anxiety is excessive and exaggerated, but it is impossible to switch off. If the anxiety becomes severe, it can take a toll on schoolwork and social life.

People with GAD often experience physical symptoms such as headaches, difficulty swallowing, fatigue, and muscle tension. Mental symptoms may include irritability, restlessness, and trouble concentrating.

GAD generally begins with ordinary levels of anxiety that increase and spiral out of control. The specific causes are unknown, although GAD tends to run in families. Symptoms often emerge during the teenage years. Women are twice as likely to suffer from GAD than men. According to the NIMH, about 6.8 million adults in the United States suffer from GAD.

Panic Disorder

People with panic disorder live in fear of panic attacks—sudden bouts of intense fear. During a panic attack, an individual may experience a pounding heart, dizziness, difficulty breathing, a feeling of being smothered, and chills or hot flashes. Some people feel like they're paralyzed or that they've lost control. The attack subsides in ten minutes or less. Often there's no specific trigger for an attack.

Panic disorder occurs when the fear of panic attacks begins to interfere with everyday activities. People begin to worry excessively about the next time a panic attack might strike. They also tend to avoid places or situations where they've experienced panic attacks in the past. If an attack occurs in an elevator, for example, they might avoid elevators in the future. People with panic disorder may become reluctant to drive or venture out into public. Panic disorder can lead to agoraphobia–a fear of open spaces.

Panic attacks often begin in the late teen years. Panic disorder runs in families, and women are twice as likely as men to have the condition. Life changes may also contribute to the onset of panic attacks. The condition is often accompanied by other serious conditions, such as depression or substance abuse. According to the NIMH, about six million adults in the United States suffer from panic disorder.

Obsessive-Compulsive Disorder (OCD)

People with obsessive-compulsive disorder (OCD) experience uncontrollable intrusive thoughts–obsessions–that produce anxiety. These obsessions fuel compulsions, which are behaviors that people undertake in an attempt to relieve their anxiety. For example, people with OCD who are obsessed with cleanliness may feel compelled to wash their hands frequently and thoroughly. OCD sometimes involves repetitive ritualistic behavior. Maybe you've occasionally backtracked to double-check that you've locked the door. People with OCD can spend over an hour each

day rechecking, arranging, and counting things. They recognize that the behavior is not normal, but they can't help themselves.

OCD is often diagnosed during the late teen years. It runs in families and may also be a result of abnormal brain circuitry and infection by the virus that causes strep infections. People with OCD often suffer from other mental health issues as well, such as depression or other anxiety disorders. According to the NIMH, about 2.2 million adults in the United States have OCD.

Some people suffering from panic disorder develop agoraphobia—an avoidance of public places and situations that can eventually leave a person feeling trapped in his or her own home.

Social Anxiety Disorder (Social Phobia)

Social anxiety disorder, also called social phobia, goes far beyond mere shyness. People with social anxiety disorder feel overwhelming anxiety in ordinary social situations. They feel terrified at the prospect of embarrassing themselves, and they fear being judged by others or becoming the target of ridicule. For some people, the anxiety is limited to specific situations, such as speaking in public. For others, any social setting produces anxiety. They may avoid eating or drinking in public, speaking in front of groups, or being observed doing ordinary tasks. They tend to worry about social events for weeks in advance. People with social anxiety disorder may have trouble forming friendships or relationships.

Social anxiety disorder often occurs alongside another anxiety disorder or mental illness. People with social anxiety disorder are often ashamed to admit the extent of their problem, and they often aren't diagnosed until they seek help for other conditions. Social anxiety disorder often appears during childhood or the early teen years. Family history, as well as an individual's personality, affect the likelihood of suffering from social anxiety disorder. According to the NIMH, about fifteen million adults in the United States are affected by social anxiety disorder.

Specific Phobias

People with specific phobias feel extreme fear of certain objects or situations. Common sources of specific phobias include flying in airplanes, heights, enclosed spaces, open spaces, the dark, certain animals, and blood. There's even a condition known as coulrophobia, which is the fear of clowns. Specific phobias are irrational–the objects of fear pose no real threat. People with specific phobias can have reactions similar to panic attacks. They also tend to avoid situations that may trigger a reaction to the phobia. In some cases, this can severely influence daily life.

Children often develop specific phobias that fade as they grow up. Phobias developed during adolescence and adulthood tend to be more persistent. Women suffer from specific phobias more frequently than men. According to the NIMH, about 19.2 million adults in the United States have specific phobias.

Post-Traumatic Stress Disorder (PTSD)

Post-traumatic stress disorder (PTSD) occurs as a consequence of a traumatic experience. The condition was first investigated medically when war veterans returned from battle with psychological symptoms then called "shell shock." It's now known that PTSD can result from many types of traumatic situations, including accidents, assaults, natural disasters, or even witnessing a terrifying event. Violent incidents are especially likely to trigger PTSD. Symptoms of PTSD may manifest shortly after the event, or they may only begin months afterward.

People suffering from PTSD often experience flashbacks and nightmares in which they relive the traumatic event. They often feel emotionally numb and avoid people or situations associated with the trauma. People with PTSD frequently have angry outbursts or even become violent. Teens suffering from PTSD may feel guilt for not preventing the traumatic incident and develop behavioral problems. PTSD can get in the way of everyday routines.

Traumatic events affect people in various ways, and two individuals will probably react differently to the same experience. In general, women are more likely to suffer from PTSD than men. According to the NIMH, about 7.7 million adults in the United States are affected by PTSD.

chapter four

Managing Stress and Anxiety

No matter how many responsibilities and demands you're experiencing, stress and anxiety can be managed. As a matter of fact, the more effects you feel from stress and anxiety, the more important it is that you get stress and anxiety under control.

There's no single approach that will banish stress and anxiety. Similarly, different techniques work for different people. One person may benefit from participating in tai chi; another might find relief in a hobby such as fixing up an old car. Either outlet provides an opportunity to relax and take a break from the pressure.

In addition to identifying ways to reduce stress, you should try to eliminate bad habits and poor coping strategies that make things worse. Don't resort to drinking, smoking, or overeating. Try ending caffeine use because caffeine can worsen anxiety. Don't take out your stress and anxiety on the people around you. Don't push away your family and friends—cutting yourself off from others will only make your situation worse.

A Healthy Lifestyle

Maintaining a healthy lifestyle can help reduce the effects of stress and anxiety. Physical and mental health are interrelated. Just as mental stress produces physical symptoms, taking good care of your body can help reduce psychological distress.

Make sure that you eat a healthy diet. A diet that includes regular meals and incorporates plenty of fruits and vegetables will provide nutrients vital to mood, energy, and brain health. Stress tends to deplete levels of some vitamins and minerals in the body, including vitamins A, B, and C, as well as calcium, zinc, and magnesium. A balanced diet will replenish such nutrients, some of which also help regulate levels of neurotransmitters in the brain. A few examples of stress-reducing foods include whole

A nutritious diet and regular meals can promote good mental health. Good family communication can also help parents understand the issues in their teen's life.

grains (such as oatmeal, barley, and whole-wheat bread), oranges, leafy greens, brightly colored vegetables (such as winter squash and red bell peppers), avocados, fish containing omega-3 fatty acids (such as salmon and tuna), nuts, and lean sources of protein. Eating junk food high in sugar and fat will just make you feel worse.

Exercise is a great way to reduce stress. It also boosts mood and benefits the immune system. When you exercise, the activity increases levels of certain neurotransmitters in the brain in a way similar to that of antidepressants. A workout also gets the physical systems of the body moving–the circulatory system, respiratory system, and other systems involved in the stress response. Consequently, these systems are better prepared to deal with stressors in the future. Exercise also relieves muscle tension caused by stress.

It's important to get enough sleep. Teenagers need about nine hours every night, according to the National Sleep Foundation (NSF). A good night's sleep slows down the production of some stress hormones. Besides, a lack of sleep negatively affects memory, judgment, alertness, concentration, and problem solving. As a result of inadequate sleep, you might find yourself functioning poorly throughout the day and feeling more stressed out, which may lead to you staying up late to get things done. Adequate rest can break the cycle.

Taking It Easy

When stress keeps you tense and keyed up much of the time, you have to make a conscious, committed effort to relax. Certain relaxation exercises can help ease physical stress. Taking time out for leisure and social activities can help you unwind from the pressures of schoolwork and family expectations. Some schools provide resources for helping students handle stress. Be sure to check if your school has any such programs.

There are a number of relaxation techniques that can reduce feelings of stress and anxiety. Deep breathing can alleviate many of the physical symptoms of anxiety and panic attacks. Once you've made a habit of practicing deep breathing,

Relaxation exercises such as yoga help manage stress and anxiety by promoting mindfulness—a calm sense of awareness of the present moment.

you can use the method to calm down quickly in situations when the stress response kicks in. Stretching and muscle relaxation techniques can relieve the muscular tension of stress. Some people practice yoga, tai chi, or meditation to relieve physical stress and clear the mind.

Make sure that you take time out every day for activities you enjoy. Spend some time listening to music or take up a new hobby.

You should also take advantage of the emotional support of friends and family. It's important that you don't isolate yourself when you're feeling stressed. Talking about what's on your mind will help you unwind and work out your worries. Support groups can also provide help and give you the opportunity to connect with other people dealing with stress and anxiety issues. Your school, hospital, family doctor, or mental health clinic will be able to supply you with information on finding a support group.

Taking Control

In addition to maintaining a healthy lifestyle and taking steps to cope with the symptoms of stress, you need to analyze sources of stress and how you handle them. People experiencing stress and anxiety tend to assume the worst about any situation. They also tend to underestimate their ability to handle stressors. You need to take a step back and realize that you can manage the responsibilities in your life. You won't be able to eliminate the sources of stress, but you can control your sense of perspective.

Start by getting organized and managing your time. When anxiety takes hold, you might feel overwhelmed by everything you need to get done. Try making a list of tasks, and prioritize each item. If you start to feel stressed or anxious, tell yourself that you have things under control and that you have a strategy for dealing with each task one at a time. You will also have to admit to yourself that some stressors are beyond your control and force yourself to stop obsessing over them.

Plan ahead for dealing with stressful situations. If you're terrified about an upcoming oral presentation, for example, prepare well in advance. Combat irrational negative

Instead of stressing out before a test by imagining the worst possible outcome, study thoroughly beforehand and replace negative thoughts with a confident attitude.

thoughts, such as you're going to humiliate yourself, with constructive positive thoughts, such as how you've thoroughly rehearsed your material. Visualize how you're going to step up to the lectern full of confidence. Remind yourself of similar past situations in which you were successful.

In some cases, you may need to adjust your expectations. The stress of perfectionism and unrealistic high standards can impede getting a task done. If you're anxious about writing an important paper, for example, concentrate on the first step—your outline, or even just starting the opening paragraph—instead of obsessing over getting it perfect in the end.

If you master strategies for coping with stress and anxiety as a teenager, it will be great preparation for your future. Good stress management skills are crucial to leading a productive, fulfilling, and balanced life.

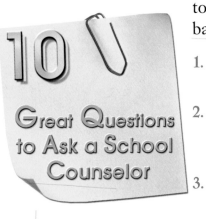

10 Great Questions to Ask a School Counselor

1. Does my school provide any resources to help students relieve stress?

2. Could lifestyle changes, such as exercising or eliminating caffeine, help reduce the stress I'm feeling?

3. How can better time management strategies or relaxation techniques help me manage stress?

4. I feel tense and worried all the time—could I have a problem with anxiety?

5. Could my feelings of anxiety be related to a traumatic experience?

6. What are the symptoms of some common anxiety disorders?

7. What anxiety disorders tend to show symptoms during adolescence?

8. What are some effective ways of treating anxiety disorders?

9. How do I find a mental health professional who can help me manage the stress I'm experiencing?

10. Are there any support groups, mental health centers, or social service agencies in my community where I can go for assistance?

chapter five

Seeking Professional Help

Sometimes the effects of stress and anxiety are too severe to deal with alone. Teens who show signs of anxiety disorders or have trouble coping with the stress and anxiety of daily life should get help from a mental health professional. People suffering from anxiety disorders are sometimes reluctant to get help. They may be ashamed of the effects of the disorder and feel that it's a personal failing because they can't control them on their own. It's important to realize that stress anxiety disorders are mental illnesses, not an indication of weakness. Anxiety disorders generally respond well to treatment, and getting help early on can improve the chances of preventing future episodes.

Seeking Help

Once you've made the decision to get help from a professional, the first step is to see a general practitioner and get a physical exam. Anxiety can sometimes be caused by an underlying medical condition. It can also be a side effect of some medications. Once your doctor has ruled out these possibilities, he or she can give you a referral to a psychiatrist, psychologist, clinical social worker, or licensed professional counselor.

Some mental health professionals specialize in treating anxiety disorders. There are also experts who focus on treating children and teens. In most cases, cognitive-behavioral therapy (CBT) and behavioral therapy are the best treatments for anxiety disorders, so seek someone with experience in those areas. No matter what type of therapist you consult, make sure that you feel comfortable sharing your thoughts and feelings with that person. An effective therapeutic relationship is based on trust, and you should have confidence in your therapist's recommendations. In addition, therapists keep their patients' information confidential: your therapist won't share your secrets and concerns with your parents.

If stress or anxiety is disrupting your everyday functioning at home, school, and work, you should consider making an appointment with a doctor or counselor.

Treatment for stress and anxiety begins with a diagnostic evaluation. Each anxiety disorder is described by specific criteria. Your therapist will ask you a number of questions about your symptoms and about your overall medical history. A diagnosis of an anxiety disorder is sometimes accompanied by coexisting conditions. A patient may suffer from more than one anxiety disorder, for example, or experience depression in addition to an anxiety disorder.

Methods of Treatment

Therapists often treat anxiety disorders with CBT or medication. Sometimes they combine both treatment methods. Treatment is tailored to the patient's specific needs. Some people respond better to either therapy or medication.

CBT involves talking with a therapist and learning specific skills that will help deal with the effects of anxiety. The "cognitive" aspect means that you address the thought processes that contribute to anxiety. Many people suffering from anxiety disorders are stuck in negative thinking patterns that cause constant fear and worry. Their minds leap to the worst possible result for any scenario. Through CBT, patients learn to consciously disrupt automatic negative thoughts and replace them with rational alternatives.

The "behavioral" aspect means that you change your reactions to the sources of your anxiety. One effective type of behavioral therapy, called exposure-based behavioral therapy, involves confronting one's fears. A patient is gradually introduced to the source of anxiety and becomes accustomed to dealing with the situation. Behavioral therapy is sometimes used alone without the cognitive element, especially in treating specific phobias.

CBT must address the specific behaviors and symptoms associated with each anxiety disorder. Patients with panic disorder learn to tell themselves that a panic attack really isn't a life-threatening heart attack. A therapist might use exposure-based behavioral therapy on someone with obsessive-compulsive disorder by encouraging him or her to become accustomed to touching "dirty" objects such as doorknobs and recognizing that no ill effects result. Someone

Several different forms of group therapy are effective in treating anxiety disorders, either combined with individual therapy or as the main treatment approach.

with social anxiety disorder may benefit from group therapy with others suffering from the condition. Patients with PTSD gradually begin discussing the traumatic event to make the memories less painful. They sometimes receive family therapy as well as CBT to help family members understand their experience and improve communication.

The outlook and recovery time varies depending on the individual and the nature of the anxiety disorder. A typical length of treatment is twelve to fifteen weeks, with noticeable improvement occurring within about six weeks of starting. Relapses may occur later in life, but they can generally be treated with another round of therapy sessions.

Medications can be used to treat anxiety disorders. They don't provide a cure, but they manage the symptoms. A course of treatment generally lasts for months or even years.

Several different types of medications are commonly prescribed for anxiety disorders. Antidepressants called selective serotonin reuptake inhibitors (SSRIs) affect the actions of neurotransmitters in the brain. Two older classes of antidepressants include tricyclics and monoamine oxidase inhibitors (MAOIs). Antianxiety medications such as benzodiazepine and buspirone target the symptoms of anxiety.

Medications take time to work, and they should be taken strictly as prescribed. If you experience any side effects, let your doctor know. If you decide that you want to stop taking an antidepressant or other medication, consult your doctor first. Some medications have to be tapered off gradually.

Both therapy and medication can be enhanced by self-help techniques. Maintain a healthy lifestyle and practice relaxation methods. Take advantage of resources such as support groups. Check out online resources as well. The Internet can offer tons of useful information (make sure that your source is reputable!) and online support communities. The Web site PsychCentral.com, for example, provides forums that welcome teens, newsletters, articles, a Find a Therapist service, and many other resources.

Teens and Mental Health

Adolescence isn't an easy time of life. It's even harder for a teenager who is dealing with a stress or anxiety disorder. Some people still view mental illness as a stigma, and people suffering from anxiety and other disorders often feel isolated. This sensitivity is especially true for teens, who want to fit in with peers. Teenagers struggling with stress and anxiety are often self-conscious about seeking help and acknowledging a mental health issue that sets them apart from the crowd.

If you have a stress or anxiety disorder, remember that there are more teens out there struggling with anxiety disorders and other mental health issues. If left untreated, anxiety disorders can interfere with school and home life. Mental health problems can even lead to suicide, which is the third-leading cause of death among adolescents, as reported by the NIMH.

Many teenagers are more willing to talk to friends about problems with stress and anxiety than to adults. Offer support and encouragement to friends who show symptoms of unhealthy stress and anxiety, and encourage them to seek professional help. Likewise, listen to your friends if they're worried about you. Those around you might recognize signs of stress and anxiety before you're ready to admit that you have a problem.

antidepressant A medication used to relieve depression and sometimes anxiety disorders.

anxiety An emotion characterized by feelings of tension, worried thoughts, and physical changes like increased blood pressure.

caffeine A stimulant found in drinks such as coffee and soda that can exacerbate symptoms of anxiety disorders.

cognitive-behavioral therapy (CBT) A type of therapy that helps people suffering from anxiety disorders change their thinking patterns and behaviors.

compulsion A repetitive behavior that a person feels driven to perform in an attempt to relieve anxiety.

depression A mental illness in which feelings of sadness, loss, anger, or frustration interfere with everyday life for an extended period of time.

generalized anxiety disorder (GAD) An anxiety disorder marked by a pattern of constant worry over many different activities and events.

neurotransmitter A chemical that carries messages in the brain.

obsess To feel preoccupied by persistent and unwanted thoughts, images, and impulses that cause anxiety.

obsessive-compulsive disorder (OCD) An anxiety disorder marked by persistent, upsetting thoughts (obsessions) accompanied by rituals (compulsions) to control the anxiety these thoughts produce.

panic disorder An anxiety disorder marked by sudden feelings of terror when there is no real danger.

phobia An intense, irrational fear of an object or situation that poses little or no actual danger.

post-traumatic stress disorder (PTSD) A disorder, often marked by flashbacks and severe anxiety, that develops after a traumatic experience.

social anxiety disorder An anxiety disorder marked by fear and excessive self-consciousness in everyday social situations.

strep Short for streptococcus, a bacterium that causes infections such as strep throat, scarlet fever, and pneumonia.

stress A physical response of the body to sudden changes in the environment.

stressor A stimulus that causes the stress response.

type A personality Someone who has a temperament marked by excessive competitiveness and ambition, an obsession with completing tasks quickly, little time for self-reflection, and an overwhelming desire to control situations.

American Academy of Child and Adolescent Psychiatry (AACAP)
3615 Wisconsin Avenue NW
Washington, DC 20016–3007
(202) 966-7300
Web site: http://www.aacap.org
The AACAP is a professional medical association dedi-
cated to treating and improving the quality of life for
children, adolescents, and families affected by psychiatric disorders.

American Institute of Stress (AIS)
9112 Camp Bowie West Boulevard #228
Fort Worth, TX 76116
(682) 239-6823
Web site: http://www.stress.org
The AIS is a nonprofit organization that imparts information on stress reduction, stress in the workplace,
effects of stress, and various other stress-related topics.

Anxiety and Depression Association of America (ADAA)
8701 Georgia Avenue #412
Silver Spring, MD 20910
(240) 485-1001
Web site: https://www.adaa.org
The ADAA promotes education, training, and research for
anxiety, depression, and stress-related disorders.

Canadian Mental Health Association (CMHA)
1110-151 Slater Street
Ottawa, ON K1P 5H3
Canada
Web site: http://www.cmha.ca

The CMHA promotes the mental health of all and supports the resilience and recovery of people experiencing mental illness.

Health Canada
Address Locator 0900C2
Ottawa, ON K1A 0K9
Canada
(613) 957-2991
Web site: http://www.hc-sc.gc.ca
Health Canada is the federal department responsible for helping the people of Canada maintain and improve their health.

National Institute of Mental Health (NIMH)
Science Writing, Press, and Dissemination Branch
6001 Executive Boulevard, Room 6200, MSC 9663
Bethesda, MD 20892-9663
(866) 615-6464
Web site: http://www.nimh.nih.gov
The mission of NIMH is to transform the understanding and treatment of mental illnesses through basic and clinical research, paving the way for prevention, recovery, and cure.

Web Sites

Due to the changing nature of Internet links, Rosen Publishing has developed an online list of Web sites related to the subject of this book. This site is updated regularly. Please use this link to access the list:

http://www.rosenlinks.com/TMH/Stress

Bellenir, Karen, ed. *Mental Health Information for Teens*. 3rd ed. Detroit, MI: Omnigraphics, 2010.

Elliott, Charles H., and Laura L. Smith. *Overcoming Anxiety for Dummies*. Hoboken, NJ: Wiley, 2010.

Hipp, Earl. *Fighting Invisible Tigers: Stress Management for Teens*. Minneapolis, MN: Free Spirit Publishing, 2008.

Hyde, Margaret O., and Elizabeth H. Forsyth. *Stress 101: An Overview for Teens*. Minneapolis, MN: Twenty-First Century Books, 2008.

Kennedy, Brian, ed. *Anxiety Disorders*. Detroit, MI: Greenhaven Press, 2010.

Lawton, Sandra Augustyn, ed. *Stress Information for Teens*. Detroit, MI: Omnigraphics, 2008.

Parks, Peggy J. *Anxiety Disorders*. San Diego, CA: ReferencePoint Press, 2011.

Tompkins, Michael A., and Katherine A. Martinez. *My Anxious Mind: A Teen's Guide to Managing Anxiety and Panic*. Washington, DC: Magination Press, 2009.

Wehrenberg, Margaret. *The 10 Best-Ever Anxiety Management Techniques: Understanding How Your Brain Makes You Anxious and What You Can Do to Change It*. New York, NY: W. W. Norton and Company, 2008.

Wehrenberg, Margaret. *The 10 Best-Ever Anxiety Management Techniques Workbook*. New York, NY: W. W. Norton and Company, 2012.

Wroble, Lisa A. *Dealing with Stress: A How-to Guide*. Berkeley Heights, NJ: Enslow Publishers, 2012.

Zeidner, Moshe, and Gerald Matthews. *Anxiety 101*. New York, NY: Springer, 2010.

About the Author

Jason Porterfield is a writer and journalist based in Chicago. Some of the books he has written for young adults include *How to Beat Social Alienation, Ritalin: A Difficult Choice, Frequently Asked Questions About College and Career Training,* and *Doping: Athletes and Drugs.* He was a peer counselor at his high school and helped his class-mates tackle stress and anxiety issues.

Photo Credits